AF237388

elena wolters

a book:

of her
oceans, forests, chambers and castles.

poetry

Bibliografische Information der Deutschen Nationalbibliothek:
Die Deutsche Nationalbibliothek verzeichnet diese Publikation in
der Deutschen Nationalbibliografie; detaillierte bibliografische
Daten sind im Internet über http://dnb.dnb.de abrufbar.

© 2020 elena wolters

Herstellung und Verlag: BoD – Books on Demand, Norderstedt

ISBN: 978-3-7534-4328-7

for all the souls that feel too much

and not enough,

that break in times of pressure.

– you will rise out of the ashes –

I N T R O D U C T I O N

the writing part was easy

painful and exhausting and heartbreaking

but also healing, reviving and cleansing

a little bit like therapy

and i like that.

deciding on what and how to share that though

was difficult.

and getting ready to share,

that was the hardest part.

if this book can give you anything,

anything at all

[and i sincerely hope it can]

it was worth the tears and doubts and crises.

thank you for choosing to read it.

TRIGGER WARNING

the pieces and poems i put together in this book

were written throughout

all different kinds of stages in my life.

that doesn't contain just the bad & ugly

or just the good & beautiful

it contains all of that and everything in between.

therefore, it is only fair for you to know

that several pieces relate to sensitive content

such as

sexual assault

violence

death

mental health

self-harm

blood

trauma

W O R D S   O F   A D V I C E

this may just be a personal preference

but whenever i read

or write

poetry

i use my voice

because although written words

are quite powerful within themselves

saying them out loud

brings them to life.

if you are able to

please

try to read aloud.

born in the ocean
grew up in the woods
waves of emotion
blossomed through childhood

trapped in her chambers
made them chambers of art
this is her castle
and this is her heart.

THE OCEAN

There are too many things i didn't want to say
too many things i really didn't mean that way
and still too many things left unspoken
like a frozen ocean my words keep holding
on, waiting
for the ice to break open
to spout
out of my mouth

but i keep cool, i keep them inside
i don't want to be vulnerable, so i keep the ice

i mean
what would i be?
without all my words living in me
what
and who would i be?

i can't live without them
they keep me alive
letting them out would equal a knife poking
my heart
waiting for me to
fall apart

what else would create those
nonexistent conversations at night?
what else would keep those loved conversations alive?

- nothing

there would be silence filling
my head and i,
i would be dead.

Our hearts still young
untouched – unfree
with hearts of gold
we reached the sea to
set the rain on fire
to let the sails admire
what wind does
as the sun breaks
with our breakdown
'cause the sea lives
         in us.

and on ships we go
straight into the horizon
and we touch
until we're touched and free
and eventually
there is
a spark
of fire

    and as we admire

our reflections in the dark
we do not see
the sea tore us apart

and on ships we go
shipping straight into the horizon
i'll go down with you
i will drown with you.

      but eventually

we keep our heads above the water.

our fire is not over.

You are still dancing
a will as strong as fire
you dance and dance and dance and dance
a forest fire's desire

as your base keeps caressing my tongue
whilst you take all your turns
your flames climb higher and higher
and i start to burn

my lips react
like purest alcohol
they burn they burn
          oh come and speak
my dearest soul

your stage starts to tremble
as my mouth starts to mumble
you are still dancing
i am still burning
we wind each other up
and you leave the scars.

with grace and rage
you spin around
with beauty placed on every edge
we make a crackling sound

exhausted
burned
little salty raindrops
reach the ground
of fire

half dead we are
half alive we stay.

we couldn't help but breaking down
when we took the jump
           and failed
we couldn't help but breaking down
because of what we never got to say.

I fall in love way too fast
with people and dreams and ideas and thoughts
i'm still holding the past
like it had a vast
impact on what's to come next
my mind is more than a complex net
of feelings
i get caught in every day
i am still in here because i can't find a way
out of
this hole, this bowl of emotions, i explode
inside every now and then
i can't control these lies i'm telling myself
i get lost every time
because i fall in love way too fast
i get lost every time
'cause i'm still holding the past

oh please,
don't look at me like that
and don't tell me all these things
because i won't forget
i will keep your words and your looks
i will keep them, 'cause they warm up my heart
and god it is so hard to let go again
to let you go, my good old friend

so please,
don't talk to me like that
i fall in love
way too fast
and i will hold the past

and the past
hurts a little too much.

She likes to pour some ink
into the boiling water
so that her burning scars turn black
and she into a writer.

I know it's not right
you are standing just next to me
so – SO far away
i want you closer

but you're unreachable.

If only i could draw
water with my words

i drowned us both in oshhhhhhheans
and let rain drrrrrip drrrip drop down onto our heads
we heard the sea-gulls uh- uh_
flap flap flapping their wings
our fingers rip-p-p-p-p-p-pled on the surface
as we turned and turned and turned
and our hearts would b-e-a-t
so – fast – and – con-tent
[SMILE] our laughs filled the salty air
before we vanishhhhhhhed with the waves

mermaids are splashhhhhhhhing with tails
and we smile at each other

SILENCE

the world is quiet
all we hear is water drrrrrip drrrip dropping somewhere above
like star showers invading the sea
and all i see are your
blurry sunlit eyes
your brightest smile

we let go
of all the air inside our lungs
and in bub bub bubbles
it leaves
leaving us empty
           so fulfilled
under the sea

oh if only
i could draw water with my words

i drew the oshhhhhhhean
for you.

I don't want you to feel bad
or even guilty
for what you did to me
but i want you to feel bad
and so fucking guilty
for what you did to me.

I wish it was us

> *to be the dancing girls*
> *in floral summer dresses*
> *sunkissed noses*
> *and with windswept sea salt hair*

i *dreamed* that it was you and i
but that i never told you.

Do not go into the sea
if you don't know how to swim

the waves are a pretty thing to look at
but beauty
and rage
lie beneath the surface

and if you're not ready
to dive and drown
with all your heart
everything you'll sea
is death – taking
your breath
away.

Why don't you understand?
it is love that i am after
your love
i don't want it
if you can only give it, when i am asking for it

i am
after your *free*
unconditional   love

i am terribly aware
that some things
are just not made for me.

I trusted you
told you everything
every single thing
about my dreams and visions
my feelings and fears

and you made sure that
every single one of them
came true.

Seeing you
being perfectly fine
after my breakdown
makes me wish something hit you
once i hit the floor

afterall
you were the one letting me down.

Sometimes they make you choose
between love
and love
ridiculous, really, isn't it?

my heart really is quite tired
because it doesn't want to choose
and it cannot
therefore, i let it follow both
tearing itself apart.

She is hot
explosive
undiscovered passion lies within
and yet
i have to keep my distance
she makes it hard for me to breathe
i have never been good with heat.

Let the clouds rise and reign
let the light collide with heaven's shine
let it rain
let the water pour from right above
make me stop

-

-

-

clap your hands
so that thunder rules my heartbeat
wave your arms
so that wind becomes my breath
open up the clouds
make the water-fall so that my tears become drops and the
drops become tears
open up the clouds
clap your hands and move your arms
make my dead, dead body dance
in nature's stage light
let my heart cry and my feet fly
make my eyes burn and my head turn
turn me into art

wash me
clean me

until there is nothing left.

Your leaving left me
with the absence
of light
and warmth
of feeling safe
you left me
with hunger and thirst
your leaving left me
with the absence of home

so i sit by the sea
and as it turns dark and cold
i slowly turn myself
into absinth itself.

Death
or the absence of life
transforms rips into cages
to keep the longing hearts from following
our newborn angels.

I know it is hard to understand
that my happiness is blinded by angst
        you have never met these demons
you could not understand

how even when i'm dreaming
when my mind is flooded by
bluest oceans, calmest seas
even fish and cancer in me feel the urge to flee,
to run to safer land
and whilst you actually belong
to mother earth's grounds
i belong to ocean's depths

angst though
it keeps me imprisoned
somewhere i am unable to breathe
you
you could not understand
your home is land.

You taught me how to swim
and now you are drowning yourself

you lost your glasses in that storm
and you forgot that vision
does not unblur
under the surface
not when the liquid stings
in your eyes and insides
you taught me to never enter waters
that i don't know the contents of

but isn't that what you have done?

you taught me how to swim
but never how to handle
seeing someone drown
that doesn't want
to be saved.

I feel like rose
ready to jump
quite literally
on the edge

but for me
there's no one to pull me back.

Tell me
do you ever imagine
you and i collide*?

       *like waves that build up tension
       until they intertwine with one
       another creating sparks
       flying high held up by
       wind for the sun
       to shine through with bright daylight
       they only could make the moon rise.

tell me
do you ever see that in your dreams?

Might be a good actress
for   dramatic
pieces

give me a mirror
i'll cry.

We were running up
and down
these hills of
grass and soft petal flowers
i held your hand
and heard
the birds' most mesmerizing song
when i dragged you along
cliff's edge

distant applause
coming from waves
crashing along the shore
longing arms of joy
they tried to bless or hearts

oh how blessed we'd already been.
only they didn't know.

finally
the net of wood and metal
underneath our feet
allowed to see how far we had come
far below
the raging waves – if only they were allowed on land.
we were safe.

and we followed the flower alignment
under sun's bluest sky

      and we stopped
      and time stopped
      just the wind   rippling through
      your wooden hair

      and when we stopped
      and time stopped
      you were holding my hands
            pulling me close
      so close
            i could not know
      whether it was the water
      the wind or your breath

      that send showers down my back.

it was just you and i
(the waves, the wind, the sea and the sky)
it was just you and i
standing within the wind's flower tide

What's the point of your shouting?
but if it truly does
bring you peace
at least one of us
can be calm.

I can see you standing in my doorframe
sleepy faces
messed up hair
i can see you waddling towards me
tired voices
all four feet bare

as you snuggle up beside me
left and right you keep me warm
i put all three of my big blankets
on top and tug us in

it's silent
just us and our three cuddly rabbits
it's quiet
as we close our eyes
i hold you tight
until all three of us can find
a rhythm
to unite in
gentle breathing, little snores

until the sun shows
upon the blue horizon
to find us snuggled up so close.

born in the ocean
grew up in the woods
waves of emotion
blossomed through childhood

trapped in her chambers
made them chambers of art
this is her castle
and this is her heart.

THE FOREST

You make me so uncomfortable
why did you tell me
you still cared
when you didn't

you knew
my heart couldn't take that
kind of falling

and yet here i am
loving you   still
like a fool
and you don't even look at me no more.

Intriguing, is it not?
how your lips don't tremble at all
the same smooth transition
between skin and tongue and teeth
whilst you form the letters
whilst you form the innocent letters
into a great, great
flawless

lie.

Maybe
just maybe
you do not like the butterflies
because it is scary
how   much
beings
change

once they leave their old shell.

it scares you to see
them free to fly
and then to see them fly
carelessly
as if they had never loved
as if they had never lived
before

as if they had never known *you*.

Life as a flower
she soon found out
was harder than it looked like

especially between those rocks
that all kept building this one
big, grey
tower.

Probably the only light that works
constantly
without the sun's warmth
water's movement
the whoosh of the wind

some people are incredibly
environmentally friendly.

I *love you*
what a wild thing to say
while touching another one's back
pulling them closer to you
posture, posture
chin up
placing your lips on hers

your hands are covered in paint
art you call this
a portray

let at least me call it betrayal.

Just like a fairy
you were floating through
fields of flowers and glass
glitter and grass
that glow made you look soft
almost fragile

oh i hope these sky-blue eyes
will never have reason to cry
sad   tears

that smile on your face   *is*   sunshine

the day you left
was the day clouds arrived

you're someplace else now
        making flowers blossom.

Just because i talk
to people you don't like
i don't like you any less.

i need you to know,
to understand
this.

She rose high
aiming for the sun
they stabbed her neck

and she continued to grow.

You are so much of yourself
your name turned into a whole ass brand.

i wish you knew
how everybody's striving to be
just a little bit
like you.

You're lonely too
i can see
i communicate
as well as i can
but i am   so
tired

i just need to sleep.

to sleep.
there is nothing i want more than that
everything feels so heavy
my chest, my legs, my back,
my head, my tongue
even my eyelids

i just want to rest.

but i also want to give you
the best   i can.

that is not what i am doing though.

everything feels so heavy.

you look at me with lost love in your eyes
and i, your only hope,
am failing you.

I AM SO SORRY
i cry

i want to jump   fly
my legs feel so heavy
i can't.

and then there is you
who i love   so much
and you can't fly
so i stay
i want to
couldn't just leave.

i cannot give you
all that you deserve.

i try so hard
i try so hard
i try so hard

but i have nothing to give you
other than my love right now
i am so sorry
i am trying
so hard

for you.
please, forgive me.

She was kept on that windowsill
next to lonely vera
blooming
once a year.
green - for all the rest of it.
but it was not jealousy
colouring her body,
hope it was
belief.

she saw the years passing by
children being born
and children growing up
boys and girls
falling for boys and girls
she witnessed first
and last
kisses
passionate hugs and tearful goodbyes
for all her life
she was stood on that windowsill

until one day

the parents died
man and woman broke down
to boy and girl
they broke down to children
that with every part of their body
cried.

she had seen years passing by
lonely vera had thirstily died

furniture was moved
the floor was vibrating
change
until she was last
to be stood in the room

when they came
to say their farewell
they looked at her

you may go
boy and girl whispered
children
they dug a hole in the ground
carefully
putting her in to cover her
with fresh
vivid soil.

in that very second
she grew
roots clenching the ground beneath
and even though it was september
she blossomed
rose high   into the air.

how come you survived?
i had never seen this kind of sorrow.

Let me walk this route
again
and again
and again

let me walk *your* route again
just once more i want you
to call my name
to call for me to wait
so we can walk our route

together.

I was walking with sharks
and when jokingly i asked
for velociraptors
i came to see that i control this world

i had not always seen that
so i shut the doors of that bus
right in front of your face
to keep myself safe

i should have saved you
because you did not deserve to die
see, your mum and thousand others had lost
their heads
to bloody swords that night

see, if only i had seen
that reasoning with some of them
could have saved these trails of red
the plants had kept them fed

see, if only i had seen
that i control the world we're in
i could have turned us into birds
and off we'd been

see, if only i had seen
that there was no need for me to be
on that raptor's back to not
end up a snack

we would have been fine
none of us had died
but see, i did not see that
not until the very end

i was walking with sharks
and when jokingly i asked
for velociraptors
they clicked open my eyes.

Cutting toxic people out of your life
is good
valid
and totally okay
cleanses your soul, mind and heart

but dragging on
instead of just letting it be
and leave it at peace
makes you
a toxic person.

The rain will stop
and the sun will break through
but until then
you have to accept that
she alone won't help you grow.

Being different is not a sin
and not to be
doesn't make you a saint.

I don't ever see flowers
or beings of any kind really
upsetting each other
just because they got up on the wrong petal

be the flower
and if you feel like saying something mean,
just because they said it first
don't.

Imagination is not the limit
it gives you comfort
when you're not feeling quite right
wings when you feel like your feet are
tied
to the ground
it gives you the freedom   you long for in enclosing times
and it brings the light.

no,
imagination is not the limit.
it is the magic within you
that keeps your heart alive.

It's true
you are
a fraudulent snake
rather
i am a foolish child
your skin looked like gold
i trusted your eyes
but they were just made up.

i should have trusted your tongue
it got split when you cut the truth
from what you were claiming to have done.

You were my sun
and even though everybody
kept telling me to put on
some sort of protection

i didn't.

afterall, you brightened my day,
warmed up my face.
such kindness couldn't be dangerous, right?

well it was.
and you burned me
right to the ground.

How could i even think
i would ever not care?

when I let you carve your name into my body, mind and soul.

Body positivity they say
after thinning their waist
and adding some boob.

You try to take away what's mine
again
when you already have
all i could give.

You will find me
in the ash tree grove
wondering why
so far away from the sea
i feel so content

when you never left your gloves.

Despite all these warnings
all around her
they kept playing with matches
to set her in place
until she was set
on fire

ready to burn them down

to the ground
where they belong

for she would rise
scarornamented wings would take her high
she would rise
and sprinkle ashes
leaving behind
a dark glowing tragedy.

She slid along her veins
she had run out of words
long before all of this had started

still that urge
to set free
stayed

the pencil drew red flowers
on that
porcelain skin of hers
wasn't she blossoming?

it's just
technically
dandelions
are no flowers

with the wind
they'll fade away
but not set free.

Sunday vancouver night
the sun set late today
tears raining form their faces
you hear them falling
on the other side of the world
mid-day
this won't stay the same
forever
it's cold
summer is over now.

born in the ocean
grew up in the woods
waves of emotion
blossomed through childhood

trapped in her chambers
made them chambers of art
this is her castle
and this is her heart.

THE CHAMBERS

It is hard
to have your heart
broken by
nothing but your own
imagination
your own tendency towards
perfection

it is hard
to have your heart broken
by no one
but yourself

1| **S**et some expectations
high and great
make sure your heart is true
and lives by them

2| give
everything you have
and trust.
all in.

3| watch.
and wait.

4| soon enough you will find yourself
on the floor
not quite whole
not quite sane

5| people you see
usually don't live by
what they themselves expect

and it is dangerous to expect
any different.

Heavy breath
she climbs up the stairs clinging
to the banister
just then her will to live had vanished her
heart had stopped beating
it's bleeding
down on all fours
she crawls
into the shower
the weak arm of hers reaches up
to turn down the tears
and cries

and as it pours down on her
eyes turn black
and her dress turns clear
the weight is pulling her down
it's drowning in own in-hales

her face all white
red patches
wet eyes watch the
hands shaking
knees breaking her heart feels SO
heavy

opening her mouth
water drowns
the sound of the breathtaking shout

help

if only she was allowed a knife right now.
being so terribly conscious
all the goddamn time
is what keeps her alive.

I try to keep it golden
but i have to stick with silver
when it comes to
colouring my skin.

I bite my lips
too much
nervousness the doctor said
but that's not true

i try to form words
to speak to you
but they're not right
you don't deserve these words of failure

i know that i am not enough
but still i try
to please your heart
even if that means to stop myself from speaking.

Funny
how you used to text me
every single day
and night
to tell me how proud you were
proud of me
and the delicacy within my fingers
within my heart

i have shrunken
i am no more
than skin and bones on floor
that with trembling fingers try
to make art

how dare you break my heart like this

the only delicacy now
lies within the tears
rolling down my bloody cheek.

The nights are taking over
        i wake up, parts of me are gone
how can i stay awake when there is a chance to be
with you
        i fall asleep and wake up crying
it wasn't you that i saw

but i will try again
        and cannot wait until night falls
don't even need to
        because the nights are taking over.

Pour me some gin
pour me some tonic
try to make me speak.

Will you look at that?
you made it into her sacred place
onto her peace
of paper.
she was planning on that anyways –
but you were supposed to make her bloom

all you did was make her bleed.

Do you ... like me?

sure! i actually have a big fat crush on you, haha

i think about you
day and night
imagine what it might
feel like
if your lips touched
mine
want our fingers to
gently intertwine

i think about you whilst i'm awake
and asleep
i try to tell myself to
feel
less of what i feel right now
but really i cannot make
my heart stop beating
for you.

just kidding! i just

love you.

oh.   oh.

I could see myself
moving my hand towards your face
tucking hair behind your ear
your breath a gentle, shallow wave of air.

i could feel myself
wandering closer towards your body.
your dark eyes glowing
hand ready to copy mine.

i could hear myself
whispering wishful words of praise
grateful you kept listening.

but in the end
my hand never moved
and yours never copied
i never came closer
mouth only opened by speechlessness
caused
by the alluring beauty
right in front of me.

and in the end
all i dared taking
in
was the sound of your breath
a gentle, shallow wave of air.

Most of the time
my dreams are cinematic masterpieces
lighting, speech and dialogue
scenery, emotion, soundtrack
characters, development
flawless
high definition and high quality

one-time experiences
that give me
all i could ever want

even you
at times
they even give me you.

3am writings are powerful
pretty and messy and
dramatically poetic.

quite difficult to read though
once the sun
takes away the starry sky.

too good to be true
too powerful to be read
their time has not come

not yet.

but continue
scribble ink on parchment fragments
and let the stars take over
when the bell tolls

it will all work out
and you *will* be allowed
to read
and to speak,
to take in 3am writings.

Would you look at this glorious tragedy we put ourselves in

if we weren't actually dying
i swore Shakespeare put us here.

Keep trying to undo me
keep trying to unknot

those bubbles won't help you

my lies are waterproof

you will need something stronger
to wash me clean.

When i say i miss you
i really miss it all

i miss our trips to nursery
with music
and your voices in the car

i miss bath time tuesdays
with extra stories
and blue & green coloured water

i miss the *are you dressed yet?*
and the *please, can you get dressed now*

can i take my bed to school?

terribly sorry, but no, you can't.
but why it is so warm and comfy!!!

i miss the *breakfast is ready!*
the *chop, chop, let's go!*
i miss the *gosh we're late!*
the *are you ready to go?*

i miss world book days
and penguin habitats
i miss rainbows, karate, swimming and gymnastics
i miss the playgrounds

i miss your first snow
and winter and christmas at the palace.

i miss your snotty noses and cold little feet
hot chocolate with marshmallows
and warm apple crumble with cream
i miss curly-whirly straws
and the way you tipped over the cups
i miss seeing you grow up
because suddenly, you made your own breakfast.

i miss sir scallywag & the highway rat
i miss introducing you to
the most magical place
i miss your christmas plays
and christmas songs
i miss your songs in general

i miss decorating the tree
and you writing the calendar story
i miss edith, zsha and tixxy

i miss your stories & lego buildings,
your theories about life and love
and god.

i miss your own choice in outfits
with christmas jumpers in july
and shorts in december
but remember it's
okay, because i am wearing my sister's tights!

i miss picking you up
and other children shouting
look, your mummy is here!
and you rolling your eyes
you had told them so many times
before
that is not my mummy, that is elena!!
i miss you running towards me
with little feet tapping on ground
i miss you jumping up
so i could take you into my arms

i miss fancy dinners
and sports suppers
little wine glasses
cleaning your teeth
and racing you upstairs

i miss bath time hairstyles
and *the first to be in their pjs wins*
i miss you choosing stories
and me begging to read the highway rat
again
i miss you getting up
because you *really* needed a drink
but really you didn't want to go to sleep

both of us knew that.

i miss you sitting on my shoulders
whilst we looked up into the night sky
fireworks exploding
stars would ignite

i miss snow days
and sledging and snowball fights
i miss snowman building
and icicle finds

i miss looking for fossils
right by the sea
miss the wind in your hair
and little, wet feet

i miss running through fields
and forests
and walks through the maze
i miss hide and seek behind trees

i miss your gemstone museum
your get well soon cards
i miss our nerf gun fights
and your living room headstands

i miss spellings
and counting,
you learning to write
and *7 x 5 makes 35*

i miss your monday jam sandwich
your friday afternoon snack
i miss walking through streets with buckets
and dressed up as spiderman and two cats
i miss the fireplace
the fish that one day were gone
the kittens from next door
and when you tried to leave the tv on
for longer than we said

i miss our clapping games
and how you put your cutlery
different people do it different ways
i miss seeing smiles upon your faces

i miss matilda
the songs and you in the show
i miss human guitars
and the way you made my heart grow
whenever you smiled and laughed
whenever i had reason to be so incredibly proud
and that happened quite often, you know?

i miss when subconsciously you reached for my hand
or turned to make sure i was there

i miss the dinosaur bowl
and the dancing mice cup
i miss your highchair
and the tablecloth world map

i miss rugby
and you falling asleep on my lap
i miss football
i don't really miss us on the train with you throwing up
but i miss holding your hand
hugging you tight
my only task to make you feel alright

i don't miss your tears
because i wouldn't want you to be sad
but i miss being able to give you some comfort
and i miss being there for you
being someone you trust
i miss cheering you up.

i miss sitting right beside
your little bed
holding your hand whilst we read.
i miss staying with you to sing you to sleep

i miss your footsteps in the morning
the way you crawled into my bed
i miss your warm embraces
the way your heads fit into my neck.

i miss all of that and maybe even more
and i need you to know that when you need me
and reach for my hand
don't be afraid to turn
pinky promise, i will be there.

Is it not disastrous?
that you cannot *make* something stay
without hating yourself for it.

It feels
as though you cut me open
and close me up
at once

it feels
as though you hold me
and let me go
at once

it feels
as though you touch me
without your body here

it feels
as though you know me
because you really, *really* care

it feels as though you love me
without it being said

this is my way to tell you
that i feel just the same.

I might be losing you
i might as well be not
but really i don't know what happens
and really i don't it want it to happen
if it means losing you.
but how could i know?
risking it
could bring the greatest prize of life
or the most terrifying loss
of all times

i don't know if i am
or ever will be
ready
enough to cope with that
you are the most
intense part of me
and my love for you
never had
will never have
an end.

i trust her though,
so this could be
goodbye.

i love you.

It feels like playing hide and seek

nobody is seeking anymore
but i cannot stop from hiding.

You do not know of my existence
even though we've briefly met

thank you – for saying the right things
even though we've only briefly met

you do not know of my existence
and still you were the one to push
me
quite gently
over the edge.

I am happy for you
i really am
but i also pity myself
i am   no longer
your only home
and you might even
forget about me

it is good to see you thriving though
you seemed lost
for quite a while
and i was not in the position
to even just slightly
change that
            none of my business.

but it is now
for i am no longer
your only home
and you, *my* only home
have moved away.

I really do like my lips
most of the time they bleed
but even when they tremble
they allow me to breathe
and speak the truth
and warmth.
even at times i'd rather not.

Today i
saw a little girl
merely ten years old
and she looked
just like you
when we
          had been best friends   forever.

i hope she keeps the ones she loves
very close and very tight
just like you did
but free.

forever only lasts so long.

do you think that *maybe*
in another universe-
we still exist?

I really like the idea
of having dinner with you
at your place
or mine
and we could cook
and eat
and do the dishes
we could have some champagne
whilst we cook
and some wine
whilst we eat

some more wine
once we've eaten
and water whilst doing the dishes

i want to ask you so many things
hear your voice
and speak to you

i guess i just really like the idea

of having dinner with you.

Every single time
i look into your eyes
i think about kissing you
and yet i don't ever do.

i never end up kissing you.

Might as well hand you a knife
makes it a bit more dramatic
when you make me bleed.

I see the way you flinch
when the clothes expose
the parts that
usually
don't show

i see the way you flinch
when your eyes explore
the parts that
not so subtly
show marks

i see the way you flinch
when the colour within my lips
changes and becomes
unidentifiable

i see the way you flinch
when my lips
edge
along the sugar-coated knife

so when you tell me you're not scared
don't act surprised
when i don't quite believe that

i know you are
and that is okay
i am, too.

born in the ocean
grew up in the woods
waves of emotion
blossomed through childhood

trapped in her chambers
made them chambers of art
this is her castle
and this is her heart.

THE CASTLE

I'm free
I AM FREE she shouts
shaking her head and shaking her hands
rattling the undone chains on her wings
touching her wrists
that chain had never exist-ed

realisation only
brought use to all her potential
now she finds herself flying.

free yourself.
don't go mental.

I want to do good
could start just *oh so easily.*

      'oh excuse me, can i help you get your bike in here?'

i want to ask the old man, clearly struggling to get his bicycle
onto the bus

      'wait, let me help you untangle this'

i want to say to the little boy whose dog's legs are tangled in
the leash

      'sorry, are you lost?'

i want to ask the woman that looks fairly confused and lonely
in the streets.

but i keep my voice down
lips parting
i breathe in

but stay quiet
i cannot do it.
i cannot.

not today.

I talk
actually
i whisper,
very calmly – i try
to explain what had happened two summers ago
and why i lied to you
why i told you things that weren't true
i whisper but my voice
breaks and tears
fill the cracks
it is unfair.

sunbeams enlighten
the driblets flying around me
clambering bones play
an orchestra
a symphony of broken dreams
a broken me
god,
will you look at how dramatically artistic this is

and i try to explain to you
what had happened
those two summers ago
i don't whisper no more
but you don't seem to hear.

i breathe in
right so
i start
all over again
desperately trying
to make my voice sound
a little more confident

no reaction
you just stare at me

and by now i am so DONE
with being SILENT

i scream, i shout at you
don't you understand?
DON'T YOU UNDERSTAND?
       do *i* not understand?

i cannot say it out loud
i,
it was me choosing location for this conversation
i cannot say it out loud
can't even whisper
i chose the *universe*
to let go of those painful words
       to not let them go
anywhere else.

If my explanation
that
[quite frankly] includes
everything you need to know
because it is everything *i* know
doesn't suffice
there is nothing more i can do for you*

*other than taking your pain for me to carry
i am sorry you don't understand

it makes everything unbearable
i just wish you could

and i don't want to tell you
it would add to your pain
but you are dragging me down
my chest feels so heavy i can hardly breathe

and i – am not the kind of person
to try and smooth the spiking air within my lungs
with liquids

i am a good swimmer
but not in liquids that make my legs cramp

water.
you should try that.

I know i could

but i can't
tell you everything.

it would break your heart.

and it has only just gained
the strength to beat again.

This does not have to make sense
to you

but that doesn't mean
it doesn't make sense
at all.

How awfully arrogant
of us
to think these grounds were our grounds

these grounds are thirsty
these forests are burning
these fish are boiling
these birds are drowning
these icebergs and ice lands are melting
next thing we know is not
the titanic hitting an iceberg
it is icebergs flooding world court
they accuse us
and there is no excuse for this

these animals are smothering
these rivers are evaporating
these rain showers are poisoned
these beings are homeless
we are taking their homes
for us

and this planet
is in extremis.

and there were streams of blood
right in front of our feet

there are streams of blood
we are in it up to our knees

how awfully arrogant
to call these grounds our grounds
humanity failed
if they were to be our grounds? why have we not taken care?
is it not enough?
to kill each other?
verbally
and actually?

do we have to kill everything around us, too?

i hope these grounds we call ours
will drown us. eventually.

We put on the greatest show
together
this is us
a thousand dreams they
come to life
another thousand die
we take each other to see the other
side

turns out i AM in a cage
towers of hope
but coated with rage
for no one
but myself
my hands could never
hold my words
i am not ready
they burn
like stars
so how would i rewrite them?
it is like running a tightrope
and all i hope is
you wait
but you turn away
from now on
you'll focus on no one
but yourself because
we would never
be enough

this *was* us.

You scarred me
then showed me
how to protect myself
taught me how to use
and how to conceal
a knife.

i hid it in my boot
and when the moment came
to expose me
you couldn't

way before then
i had learnt not to trust
the cause of scars

i am sorry draco.
this is my victory.

I want no one
but you
to leave your black leather gloves
on my shop counter
to say thank you
with lunch
when i go out of my way to return them
to say thank you
with lunch
and a life with you.

Although you talk to me
accent free

in good rhythm and flow
with easy words
not really fast
but not too slow

i don't quite understand

you don't make sense

not anymore.

Maybe you should have killed me
in that dream of mine
but you didn't
instead
you let me touch your hair
and look into your eyes
you let me compose a masterpiece
          your head on the floor
it looked so pretty
*you

and now you don't talk to me
not anymore
you should have taken that knife

and ended it
once and for all.

Blue and green are your favourite colours
maybe that's
why you felt the need to paint them
all over my heart
with your bare voice.

Wandering through
amsterdam nights
all we see is red lights
stop signs
the moon shines bright
whilst you hand me your drink
you say you want my body
to stay hy-
drated
i laugh
and so do you
we laugh so much and so loud
until our knees bend
we almost collapse when
he asks us to come
we are stumbling through
cobblestone grounds

holding our midst
we are laughing out loud

it is a very fine - almost invisible
line
that keeps together my expanding heart
in this glorious night
and whilst everything feels wrong
this
feels wonderfully right.

I have such
high expectations
for myself

day for day
i beat myself up

for not reaching those
high expectations

please don't push me any further
i can already
hardly cope.

Tie the corset
tight behind my back
i am not able to breathe,
walk or even stand straight
on my own.

For god's sake no
i do not need you in that
silly costume

i need a sword
to cut
me free
and through your throat.

One room
that we danced in
and kissed
we danced some more
and kissed again
one room
turned into one bed
and still our bodies danced
eventually we slept
together
no sex
just sleep
no sex
just sleep

and when the moon reached her full potential
we got up to dance
again
never before had we spoken
everything was silent
yet in our minds and hearts and eyes
there was the music of the night
that made
our bodies move
to carry *everything*
into fingertips and swaying hips
beating rips and pointed lips
to carry *everything*
into our legs and feet
we still carry *everything* in the way
we bleed

trembling
we stopped

final pose
lips moving still
no words said

the moon had died
tonight – she couldn't handle
everything

final pose
lips moving still
but no words said
we shall get some rest
turn the room back into a bed

tonight – she couldn't handle
everything
but she shall rise
and we shall welcome her
dancing the music of the night
together
no sleep
no sleep

one room
that we danced in
and kissed.

I thought i had found peace with you

but it wasn't the lullabies you sang
it was drugs you put be on
so subtle
i didn't even realize

then you left
and all of a sudden
not a single song seemed to work for me

i am losing my mind.

You have no right no more
to tell me that you love me
so that i come back to you

you have no right no more
to tell me you are sorry
so that i forgive you

you have no right no more
to call me out, for leaving you on unread
DON'T YOU UNDERSTAND
i didn't even want to read
another lie you came up with
so that i would speak to you again.

you have no right no more
to tell me that you're trying
so that i would stay a little longer

you have no right no more
to tell me it was wrong
because it was me.
it was always me that was wrong

you have no right no more.

I am not sure you remember me
but i
for sure
do remember you

i was not going to tell you
who i had kissed
or hadn't kissed
who i had slept with
or hadn't slept with
i was not going to tell you
my bra size or what i wear to bed

and you called me prude
a bitch

and i didn't agree to
get out of the water
to have you see my bikini
i didn't agree to paint my nails because YOU
liked it better
and i did not agree
to meet you for dinner

and you called me prude
and a bitch

i did not want to hear your stories
about how you liked 'your girls'
THEY ARE NOT YOUR GIRLS
about what you think of to get yourself going
I SAID NO
about your sister and what she looked like when she gets
undressed
I MOVED AWAY

but you kept following
and you kept speaking
when i MOVED AWAY
and i said STOP and NO

i moved into the deep
i was SO scared
35 degrees the sun was burning down
there was no protection
just two pieces covering parts of my naked body
i moved into the deep
and i wanted to drown

i remember you
and i remember what i felt like
and every time i walk into the water
i am praying to god
that you (and everybody like you) are burning in hell
and
that you (and everybody like you) are burning so badly you
cannot even move *near* the sea.

Take something
sharp
put your finger on it
gently
could it hurt you?
good
now come over here
let it dance
gently
above my skin
let it touch me
gently
you make me all nervous
why are you adding so much pressure?
gently i had said
that's right.

So? why did you not tell me before?

but darling i did.
it's just you never listen.
and i have simply stopped repeating myself over and over and
over again

and you didn't even notice that.

99 years
because her dress was ripped
her body stripped
down
hands were kept tightly together
legs were spread widely by pressure
heart and soul

bruised

99 years
because he did not listen
when she whimpered under his grip
99 years
because he did not listen
when she said no, pressed against a wall by his hips
99 years
because he did not care
that she turned away trying to break free
99 years
because he did not care
that he was making her

bleed

and she cried
and screamed
shed tried and tried and tried
to break free

99 years
because *no* just wasn't enough
99 years
because he had left her
with trauma and fear and bruises and tears
he had left her
with parts of him
and she chose

to say no

to at least that.

I am still hurting, you know?

that's right, sorry. my fault.
you didn't even know i was hurting in the first place
because you never ask me how *i* am.

sometimes petty wins me over.
in my head it does anyway.
i know what to say and i know what to do
so you'd never know
that sometimes, petty wins me over.

Spent hours and days and weeks
looking for the song that made you sing to me

i like you
broke from your lips
again and again and again

until you pulled me into your arms to state
that what the song made you say
you meant.
because you *really* liked me.

Don't make me wait
for you and what you still won't say
don't make me move
to adjust us and our damaged love
don't make me speak
to then hit my cheek

because you didn't like what i said.

it takes two
to tango
and to love

and i can't dance this on my own

but something else
i can.

She likes everything shiny
and everything sharp
everything royal
and everything dark

it holds the power that she doesn't have

crown
on top of her head
knife
behind her back
crystals
on her fingers

and a big black ballroom dress

ever so slightly
hinting
at the chaos

that lingers
behind those glowing eyes.

she hides behind the power
she physically applies.

Take me away.

away from their voices
their jokes and their eyes
away from home – that is not home anymore.
away from their harsh tones
and pressure-filled words

i cannot take it anymore

please, *beloved ocean,*
take me away.

W O R D S   O F   G R A T I T U D E

i wouldn't be able

to even just begin to

put into words how grateful i am.

i want to thank those, who helped me get this done.

thank you,

for every kind word, your support, your patience,

your honesty and critique and for your time.

and i want to thank *you*

for choosing to read this.

some people

deserve their own mention in this

<3

CAITLIN

i couldn't count all the hours you spent listening to me and my poetry, even if
i tried. you went through more than one crisis with me and managed to keep
me on my feet, when all the doubts were weighing me down.
your patience, your love and your advice, but mostly your unwavering
support made me push through and put this together. this book would not be
what it is, had it not been for you. you are a star!
i love you *so* much. thank you for staying with me - every step of the way.

HELENA BONHAM CARTER

& ALLIE ESIRI

it may seem silly to say that, but whilst i did have this dream of my own
writing put together in my own book, i didn't think i had it in me. it seemed as
though i wasn't good enough for poetry and as though i was a fool for even
just attempting to write. these thoughts & doubts stayed until i met the both
of you.
it was nothing in particular you said or did, but in that night
you allowed me to allow myself to let go.
it was the way you carried the words, the way you made them your own
it was the way you allowed them and yourself to *be*
the love i hold for you is full of gratitude and raw emotions
thank you, for helping me regain my freedom and faith,
for writing, does not make you a fool.

CLEMENTINE & WILLIAM

i am not sure you know, but you helped me to get back on to my feet.
i had no idea life could be this bright and beautiful, i had no idea i would ever
wake up thinking about how wonderful it is, to be alive.
but it is and you were the ones who showed me, every single day. thank you.
my love for you is never-ending.

MEINE LIEBE FAMILIE

danke,
dass ihr an mich glaubt, immer, in guten wie in schlechten zeiten
und dass alles bei euch sicher ist.
danke, dass ihr mir stets zur seite steht und immer mein zuhause seid.
alles gute in mir, hat seinen ursprung in euch.
ich hab euch lieb.

JENNIFER

you know what you are to me and you know no one, could replace that.
that said, i will not go into too much detail, but please know,
that your love means the world to me, you do.
you are *home*, always. even when you are so far away.

ENA

for staying with me.